BEAST

BEAST

—⁓—

Mara Adamitz Scrupe

Selected as winner of the National Federation of State Poetry Societies
2014 Stevens Manuscript Competition
by John Witte

NFSPS Press

This publication is the 2014 winner of the National Federation
of State Poetry Societies Stevens Poetry Manuscript Competition,
an annual competition with a deadline of October 15th.
Complete rules and information on the purchase of past publications
may be obtained by visiting www.nfsps.com or by contacting:

Amy Jo Zook
Stevens Poetry Manuscript Competition Chairman
3520 State Route 56
Mechanicsburg, OH 43044

NFSPS Press

Cover photo, "Adult Black Bear," by Dean Fikar
Author photo by Daniel Jon Holm, 2014
Interior and cover design by Diane Kistner
Book set in Book Antiqua

ISBN 978-0-9909082-0-3

On *BEAST* by Mara Adamitz Scrupe

We find in *BEAST* poems of relentless energy as well as hesitation, and recognize in them the halting and swerving of our lives. All the incongruous clutter of our days — the fungus and stars — weigh on the page. Scrupe's wry humor cushions the thought of our bodies "chaffed and sloughed," growing "transparent." These crowded, unflinching poems chronicle the small catastrophes and redeeming joys, the emotional commotion of life as we know it.

—John Witte, 2014 Judge

Judge's notes on the 2014 winning manuscript of the National Federation of State Poetry Societies Stevens Manuscript Competition

Table of Contents

River Musk Perfume

As for the doe leaping the barbed wire fence   catching her hoof,   hung,

hind leg shattered,   coyotes got the scent of her,   pellucid eye,

they found her.

And a couple of woozy-headed strangers,   grinning too

close,   strafed   in spotlight?   Balance *that* risk   —

or maybe,   we bargain:

River musk perfume   hot soakings   icy

downpours   the colors of eels' bellies   terrapins sheltering

in unmown fields   —   Or instead,   just

Surrender: our own personal   sainthood,   martyrdom,

our self-deceptions,   encumbrances,   limitations   —

But then,   what would we be   without them?

Chemistry

I haven't found the bottom of want the furious beating staccato

thrum   the rushing sound I carry their lives in my own in my blood

and tissue and bones dancing in the kitchen with my shoes off and when

I can't love anything, anyone, quite right ah, fuck the eyes the skin

and toes   you do that thing you cannot stop I cannot   stop

banging these pots and pans pulling the half-sun   tumbling the nighttime

in all around us ass   over teacup.

Love Letter

Think of this as a love letter, this dry-scratch
lawn a battleground.   Consider this a hats off
to Slavic despair   or better yet a bottoms up:
          last night I drank tequila and it tasted
like shit so I had another and dreamt
tar oozing my mouth   *rinse and spit*
jamming up my lungs my throat
                    rinse and spit

Think of this as   accounting   an
abnegation,   skin rubbed raw, sin a common
communion,   but grant me just give me
this: my teeth are black the teeth you
love my head wispy, bald as a grandmother's
thighs I'm withered my juices all dried

Up   —   Only listen to me: I am no cloistered
sister no barmaid no wife carefully folded cut
sewn in her winding sheet each even stitch
a blue sky a pure note a single voice.   I'm a hard-
headed piece: I crave I despair, soft and solid,
skin and skeleton   and sinew.

How Then To Discuss

Inconstancy or faithlessness or how finally it's the one
who holds your hand in the   —

    start again

Night music   the skull's shape silhouetted head
and shoulders backlit against   —

    start again

Sleepless hiss of highway   I was on my way over in
shambles   no one gets off easy in this   —

    start again

Stealing quietly into other rooms undressing I close
my eyes as soon as I   touch myself right up until   —

    start again

Dispute batters these walls   *there's* the heart's
mystery pot of gold drunk on Saki I didn't say it   but   —

    start again

If once I could beg moan tell you stories my lips pressed to your
ear why, now, can't I   —

    start again

Falling asleep   to the lilt and click of your
breath   we cast off safety, security   —

    start again

Forever songs without lyrics   —   the heart's cruelties   —   what
future?   and cheap to go with   —

    start again

Treachery is the hardest part   —   next to   answering or even   finding
courage   to ask.

Bound

1.

fly!

Whisper   tiny silk shod wings to pretty
talon   toes,

beauty betrays!

Warn   three-inch wound-
blossomed   feet.

2.

The mother can't watch,   turns away, teeters,
swaying   from the room.   Meanwhile, other women's

practiced fingers   strip and peel,

Unwind, pry and lift the rotten
digits   one by one   to ten.

3.

We are the gesture-
gatherers   the secret-keepers,   fettered

of craft,   fashioners of the venial,

the graven,   abluted, our hands soothe and
cup, like a second-sighted   seer's, tea bowls slumbering

in open palms.

Try Resistance, Defy Entropy

Tadpoles wriggling   to shore   become human.

    Chicken of the woods   (Laetiporus)   can't be pried   attached,

as it is,   fungus to tree.

Organisms evolve: structures,   cells.   Adjustments

    educe behaviors,   implications,   the universe

moves on.

       Try resistance.   Defy entropy.

      But,   I think,   *everything*

Changes.   Urgent plums drop from limbs.   Skins slit

    where they hit

the ground.   When you asked for   that

That way,   *that breach,*   something shifted

    marked me,   that afternoon's thick

white   sheets   —

Everything

Physics: the study of the physical world, the galaxies,
the night sky you wrapped your love

Around.   Over breakfast

At the fancy hotel restaurant   you chose your words
carefully: sons,   failures,   regrets.

A trip to Bayreuth over coffee.

I never took you for a Wagner man. I never took you for
disappointed.

Before you knew me   you handed me   your life.

I never returned your book   of stars.

—ᔕᔕ—

Reckonings

How casual we reckon   the heart's prejudice,
the body's truths,   as if we choose one path

And not another, love one and not   the other.

How we pass our days   metering the hours now
until morning's last solitary stars;

Illusions fill holes memory's   abandoned.

How we make our trades: a scrap of yellow
silk,   all the comely, costly things   held close

In our delight, held up   to catch   the light.

Chores

Dust speckles the bedside tables and lamps and stacks
of books and unread magazines.

We shed it

Daily minute-by-minute, and draw a finger
through to count the hours that leave

No trace.

We signify our passing incrementally,   wiping up messes   —   today's,
tomorrow's   —

Thinking the jobs well done,

Straightening the sheets,   plumping
the pillows,

Chaffed and sloughed   little by little we're

Transparent, no longer held together
in one tidy package but rubbed to water

Washing the tiled floors   clean.

Handyman

Some people never get rid of anything. Sheds full
of items too valuable to throw out, pole barns packed
to the rafters: torn screen doors, three-legged chairs, stuffed-full
bins of leftover packets: do-it-yourself screws and nuts
and bolts sure to come in handy   one of these days.

Some people have so much, they go on TV for help with the
mounds and heaps and boxes crammed so tight and piled
so high they need paths to find their living room sofas, their buried
beds and kitchen tables, their spouses leave them and their children
move out and refuse to come home until   *something is done.*

Some people find a use for everything.   Eventually. They never
let a thing go to waste. They stand and stare at the rotting steps,
the holes in the roof, knowing just how to make the best of salvaged
slates, two by fours, weather-beaten siding;   willing miracles
of reparation, like patron saints   of all things that fall   apart.

Esther's Man

One brother got the fertile soil and built the biggest

house.   Esther's man got the farm and sixty-eight cows

and the old folks' debt and the house you couldn't live in

     on the played-out eighteen acres.

Another brother poured the concrete apron around his new

house. Esther wants an apron too   —   canted concrete humbling

the mud and manure.   They gutted it and fixed it up themselves

    alright,   and Esther,   Esther made

The appointment. Clean cement right up to the front door

is what she's after when she drives into town.   But her man,

her man carries the mortgage and money's desperate tight

    these days,   *over-leveraged,*   the bank man tells her.

Without Speaking

Tonight I'll fix supper as I always do. I'll stand exasperated
in the middle of the kitchen floor,

      waiting for a message,

      some kind of sign,

beginning at the fridge or else the pantry or drifting,
undecided,   toward the shelf that holds the cookbooks,

the do-it-yourself manuals,   the glossy magazines. Tonight
I'll choose a dish a foreign name, an impressive

provenance; this I'll offer in exchange for lawns mowed and weeds
whacked, screens hosed-down,   pin-prick mildew bleached

from porch rails.   POLENTA.
Tonight we'll have   *Po-LEN-Ta.*

I'll sound the rhythm without speaking   I'll whisper it out
loud, relishing each syllable   with exaggerated

puffs of my lips   rolling it   —   once, twice   —   against the roof
of my mouth   expelling the word   with a wanton

flick!   of my tongue: *Po-len-TAAAAA!*   Corn mush, johnnycake,
hominy grits' grain-textured mass yields soft in the mouth,   pone

porridge stirred smooth, scooped out cooling on an oil-slicked
board,   homely as flesh pressed

in the night, fingertips searching,   thighs teasing
hips,   twenty-eight years   and counting.

Pretty Machine

You had her longer, rode her
harder, she let you down at least
as often, threw a rod, staggered up mountains
and off again, pushed through deserts,
loaded up now, strapped tight for the drive
to Annandale, for the man with a bleeding
ulcer which is better than a heart attack,
he wants her, though if his wife were alive,
but she's gone, a couple years now, he's adjusted
pretty well but the ulcer didn't come
out of nowhere, a peck and a quick goodbye   —
that's how we do it,   it's already afternoon,
you'll grab a sandwich on your way back,
I'll eat leftovers tonight you'll tell me
the new owner's turned his wife's house
into a shop moved in bikes in various stages
of tear-down and rebuild, Triumph triage
everywhere, work stands at eye level in the guest room
he watches TV scooting on a stool as he works,
Amal carbs line up neatly on the dining room
table, he never sits anyway but stands slouched paper
plate in one hand folded slice in the other, components
freshly painted dry on clotheslines
strung across the living room, guests still sit
on the three-cushion sofa, parts skimming past,
yours is the one he'll ride if all goes well
in Emergency, he's waited forty years
while you tore up gravel on the ALKAN,
while you camped the outskirts of Vegas   *circus,*
circus! he dreamed of three-strokes, she dreamed
new floral davenports and matching brocade
drapes, you promised groceries on your way
home,   your tread on the stairs pulls me
awake, you sit at the edge of the bed
beside me   in the dark, your lips brush
my forehead, you reach for my hand your fingers
spreading mine apart   to fit.

AM Radio

        Our compass,   steadied,   points true

north   the hard talk truth long   overdue   a plain truth of figment

and ferocious   silence: our language of decades

    and devotion.

        Years ago you drove the plains   peddling

books and bibles   town to town   Paul Harvey on the

radio   preached parables and broken

    chaff,   dust and snow and caution,   in familiar

remnant phrases.

Whiteout

This is a day for sleeted sand pelting our cheeks.

This is a place for sideways gales and broken drifts.

This is a time for no grand plans   busted wipers

slap a clumsy rhythm,   headlamps froze   bump

and skim, dead ahead, jolt and slip,   angle and plume

    and spin.

Time To Go

Years go by and you never worry if the suckers aren't
pruned   you're not on the look-out for premature
blossoms or bumblebees or signs of midnight

plunder. You recognize the dangers of anticipation,
calculating bushels and counting on long,   late-
summer days for picking, peeling, quartering, slicing.

    And then,

one especially hard winter,   you start paying
attention, you scour the Almanac for advice
concerning early snowfalls and late

frosts,   you search for signs of mishap   agonizing
over shallow roots,   frozen buds   ice laden wind-fallen
limbs   until finally,

spring arrives   and out of the blue   both trees take sick
and die, one right after the other.   At first you think, *I could have
saved them*   and then: *It was their time to go.*

Orchard

I feel our precariousness   as an exhalation before daybreak, your arm

     bent beneath my shoulder,   your crooked

Breath   against my back.   I lie awake   hearing

Them call in the pre-blue dawn,   their huffed   rasps

     in the orchard,   the whistling sighs   pushed

From their breasts,   bounding towards the woods

     and refuge.

Blows, Shadows
(Taormina)

Morning school begins with training   men and beasts

below prepare,   turn away,   look out

to sea.   Rise, first

light,   reach, blows,   glance and

quicken,   shadow-rush rock to rock, in and

out,   and between.   Elephants,

lions and tigers   hunted to extinction

for the games,   strenuous slaughters

exposed,   incised in clay in the round:

unprotected limbs,   familiar backs and buttocks limned blood

and black,

captive combatants   we can't admit

are us.

Day, Night

By *grazioso* I mean

temperance: crane-limbed women   at the park by the river

stretching   reaching   folding

spreading

By *sostenuto* I mean

pause,   pay attention,   try   I mean day, night two

instruments, interpolations thrashed out,   pedaled and

plucked and   struck   together

shifting signatures   unrelenting,   *adagio anima*

in deep duet

By *appassionato* I mean

cadence,   *tempo rubato*   keeping up, keeping time

your part,   mine.

Free

> That Paint you showed me

standing in the field where you let   the trapped groundhog

> go free?

—

> We talked   as though

we had forever   —   no seams in this earth would ever   split,

> opening,   to swallow us whole,   as though

no hidden fast flowing underground stream would sweep us   away

> unless we're very   careful.

—

> That pony you showed me?

You said: *he's wild*   because he knew enough   to keep

> his distance.

Shivaree

Some scary things some things,   some
things that sound like words but work like fists,

or cudgels if we live in dark times.
     Some things that fly

around the room striking the walls
and ceilings, splitting the plaster,   cracking, denting

Some things that seem like omens, tarred
whispers, a serrated knife cutting paper

Something that rips apart
in the middle of the night, down

The center   a seesaw with too much weight on either
end   bump-assed thud and hit the ground   —

painful surprise   —

Some things that holler and shout
and weep and fuss, that shock the mouth like salt

expecting sugar.

After Hours

Night streets keep tabs   on our movements

cigarettes corner shift and swagger smiles,   security drifts

    past obligation curbside,

        shadow-lingering   perchers,   scrap-eager

  roused late-night   by moonlight,

     restive.   Hovering

  duty shack surveyors,   phones raised

mid-phrase stalk hip-hugger lean and stroke and sway invitation

  rhythms   appraise the mouth to mouth up

close in the darkness,   in a moment   clasped

       tight,   and pushing

Observation Upright

Lacking a glass partition,   *Lord,*   *protect us*   Flying,

flailing,   help us hold   ourselves   upright,   keep still

vigil   wait to see   light-cowed

Masses   press muscles   to metal, remind us

dear God, we are not alone, preserve us from this,   our madness over-

taking us,   our hearts, mine, yours: bullhorns

bellowing,   what we need

Now is a brick house   not this frail

arrangement   —   lanterns shine   windows,   row

upon   row,

Oh Lord,   our colors   revealed   shameless   on display

amplified one next to the other;   passed from our bodies

through our eyes   in pre-set intervals in some rare system

of exposure.

That Moment We Chose

In that moment we chose our sport, play, impulse, affinity,
inclinations sprung up
around us pierced us through   caught us off guard arced us
tugged us plumb   chest to
chest our wounds most tender roused the world's ridicule but inside
they couldn't touch us, the cliché of

Us   —   it's just colors childhood Crayolas from which I drew Jesus
yellow-headed
like me,   And you   dark Pontius, you devil, you sinner,   eluded
censure   —
what could they know of that magnet   our sway
investigations   our unlikely

Sameness the creamy center we share despite the outer
cover as death our
goad our private driver asks *how much?*   our model the ineluctable
hereafter   —   must we follow no matter
what?   That halo round your stygian head   not truly
black

But never mind   my Baptist Quaker Zen redeemer
the one to repair
my broken-down parts   disregarding
past allegiances, errors, walking toward me, my arms
down, my shield   fallen away.

Steady

Heart pine floorboards
Next to the paint cans
It's been a long time since this old house's seen
Lay your jacket down on the floor has
splinters   If I could answer that   —
Will you stay   does it matter?
It's monkey-feeding time   Pat my
ass   that gesture
It's hard to think without your   —
That old song *Don't*
Explain   Would we if we
Shaking quaking all
Aquiver   Sweat-soaked hair,
hair,   Sam Cooke on the radio
I'm so glad trouble don't last
Always   I'm so glad
Odor of unwashed
This old place has seen some
What we would do if we
Murmur, promise, get ahold of
Acrid tang of private
Good and hot throw a log
On it   I'm lying here cold
Said in passing   warmed brick
If you don't want to know cover your
Daytime man, nighttime man
Serves you right early evening
Light wavy glass heavy wood
Iron latch from the inside
From trickle to bang and shudder
Accumulation and overflow
Slosh to rush drumming up against bead-board
Rhyme and flow safe for now
If you believe that sort of
Thing   You don't say   who's
Hurt   anything   to beat it   Have to
Go now   *oh* not yet,
Yet   not quite
You don't want to talk   please
Fight enough, everyday, a drink
Please, bourbon and a splash
Solid   *thunk*   steady,   now   —

Velvet

Velvet, *oh!*   frighten me,

For no one else keeps
this intemperate pace   brush past me on your way to someplace   else
look away   the flat of your hand   sliced like a

slap!

Stay me   high up on this wire   make me dread both
the plummet and the yield menace me ill from want   push me pull me
by your belly's   creasing,   cast me out   deny me brand

me   in marks the size and shape your fingertips paired assault

stigmata   of my thighs but only   steer me.

Snug Round Humming

I want to tipple you swallow you whole your slow slung
thighs,   black rivers,

Drown me in nearness,   distance me for spite crush your breath
against mine,   your soothing tongue   I want to take it

Another time   your heft outspread above me
your snug round humming singing sweating

Heedless bliss   your hands on my shoulders pushing me
down,   insist me furiously   questioningly,

Let me quaff you   fill me, pour me   make me

A pitcher,   it's your need, I need return to   slake me   thirst me
one more time at least   draw me, render me

As water from your well   my eyes your seas, whispers,
breathe me,

From your mouth to my openings smooth me break me rush me
slow me,   lift me,

Leave me   stay.

Down Ride Dream

In mine   the see-through-man's mouth makes an

    O   stripped off wet pulling me low he's   the numbed

night   the basement soil – spumed   steps

    a truncheon   I'm the driving

he's the crushing   hurtling through darkness

down   I'm the clenched sky,   the twinkled,   weeping-

without-water firmament   shake   he's the one

    hand at my back

    fist to my belly   the

It's four AM Christchurch time   *teach me the Maori*

    so I can get it   *right*   the tap-

tongue   tooth   air swoosh

    space   between your clement

extensions   ankles straight cross-

    legged   save me   straight

up, maneuver me   my back to you,   something new,   bottom

    south-sliding   smooth

    down ride.

Sugar

      Don't stop,   candy cotton spun-glass   so sweet   stop
for anything,   *please, everything,*

        Jesus Christ!   sticky greedy mouthfuls sucked
tongue to palate   juiced
      guilty tooth-achy syrupy
melting away like snow in May   sweet no matter how hard   you try to

        —

Ruptured somehow,   tore away   before we had
the chance   or maybe we didn't,   and never

        —

      Define naked: stripped   the tip of me
in the balance   that part of me   you

       say   tastes best unbathed   on all
fours licked bare knees   fist twisted hair   pull   back

       back   eye-to-eye   *you my bitch?*   down on
all   fours   shame the scent   of

               tender is   —

Slow, Wild

Again,

rapture tugs muscles   knees to thighs
to hips   to womb   arousal,   flush

and drain of love   —   Importune

me   my here, my outpost, my slow and wild one do what   you
want   curiosity wants congress   I want past
shortcuts

love love love

whatever I mean   by that,   *love counts*

everything.

—

Glancing across the table, the room,   sweet corruption
smiles,   I smile back.

Whatever bound   once,   is hardly
holding: yoked is pulled   apart.

Beast

Regular Sunday afternoon small talk,   *you know:*
insect itch and whir,   seized   airborne

shuddering   summer sylphs impale the

Bergamot blossoms   and Pinks:

I envy them.

—

At a crossroads,   the male's back arches   over
the female   momentarily suspended   reconsidering, maybe,

or demurring, after all,   or unable to do it but feverish,

Fuck-addled,   struggling.   Mounting, it's called,   but really
it's not that simple   it's   aggression and rebuff: she squirms up incisors

clamp his neck: encouragement or resistance,   *I don't know*   —

Trembling, I'm sweat-drenched shoving a mower diagonally across
a field, sinking in floodplain,   cutting the engine,

Watching.

—

Close your eyes,   picture desire: submission
and domination.   Maybe Lawrence had something, after all
the denouement between partners at best   biformed:

gentle and furious,   *carnal*   the root of *carnage,*

You know,   this thing

this long-suffering   humiliating, needful,   enjoined
beast   between us   animals with intellect   lying,
truthful,   tacit.

Little Signs Of Betrayal

On the mountainside she struggles to work the clutch while he stares out
the passenger window. That evening storms slam the coast. Sitting up past
midnight, mosquitoes harass her bare shoulders, thighs,   she listens mute
as he explains, again,   timing, his finances,   a daughter not even
in high school.   Later, lost in the dark, he sits in the passenger seat,
map folded in his lap, refusing even to look

A man balances on rocks near the sea, turns his back   slips out
of shorts and tee-shirt. In scorched light his skin reminds her of three copper
coins they'd picked out together in a tourist shop, she thinks of antiquity
climbing these rocks   how predictable and fleeting,   our demands
and explanations,   teasing, he places the conch against her ear, saying
listen,   you'll hear   —

You gave me new life. Or perhaps it went *you are life.*   Tenses, past
and present, seem important to her now, considering the gulf
between them,   as though he controls the clock, time slows, he adjusts
the lens as just then the sun makes its descent to dusk as she imagines
the slightest push sending him over the edge   past crumbling stone
cottages,   flat-soled boots skidding   on scree

Dog Days

to grasp the physical sense of *hotter than ten hells*   and *dog days*   and *just*
about the time you think you've got it licked   is to be sun-blind and flat on your

back   trying   not to question this godforsaken machine lame in a field,
this familiar path,

     its writhe and turn

muscle-roots shove right up through the soil,   just barely dark but
losing the known,   pick a profile, what the hell an outline, find and trace
its edges,   night-blind,   both the smooth and knotted course,   years
underground, the damnedest things each five eyes altogether still-blind and
digging killing slits in tree trunks,   August dry birds' mating in huge
whoring throngs, exoskeletons resonating to beat the band,   to deafen
or drive us all   to drink,

     If you surface once

in 13 years or 17 or some other prime number   would you know
     what to do or
how to act whether something had already happened to make you what you
don't want to be   but can't help living?

Where Love Goes

I would like to ask you when   when her

hips   stopped

        her breasts

I would like to know   if you met her   today

on the street   or passed her   on the sidewalk

    if you watched her   go by   today

would you turn   around   right around

                                and stare?

Now

I only know you as you are now and if I stand naked examining pressing

lumps assessing my ass in the mirror, what you see: old body liver

spots,

    wrinkles arrayed in patterns

around my eyes,   aged flesh, you know me as only I am now,   past

time

and if I fall your crooked fingers catch me   fixed in my sight,

    make a net,

    right me.

A woman decides this is enough,   enough,   and she is through and there

    will never

    ever be   more than this,   in this life.

South Philly Valentine

Unmistakable amplified street-side *I want you*

to want me   that voice salty rhythm section underfoot

crunch step hip sway Valentine's Day dusk at 5PM every

second man's arms hugging roses some sheepish if you pass

close by dodge each other's satisfied eyes that say maybe

it'll be my night like the man sings *the right way* if you want

to change my mind even daisies might do it if you're

wondering he's thinking about giving me something

precious talk me into that thing baby *baby's sharing* change

my mind *oh baby changing my mind* mirrored street-side flash and glow

tonight-light like its Saturday night light fantasia in purple rain

boots slosh and pick my way puddles day disappointing no snow

soggy ruin my new shoes day no day off day had to work gray

day but still tonight *he wants   me.*

Intimacy, Life

Young women give no quarter.

In her white lab coat, brand new stethoscope   draped
around her neck,

My feet in the stirrups knees dropped wide open,   she starts in
on treatments,   risks and cancers

Aging and intimacy,   (*this* makes her visibly squirm)

        life with it,

        life without,

Choose   one:

        appetite's slender death

        or *going out headlong, willing*

        all the way.

Sixth Great Lake

These scrabbled isles shorn   sea from shore, these bled-
          white ghosts trapped and lost
below, cold as forever, lying in their granite-slab
          beds.   These spray-hooks   upwards frozen,
mid-air,   mysterious as milk frothed solid, viewed
          from within, shrewd
as silk stored in tissue   unfolded once,
          with a *whish*   —   Years later,
same shore, same inland sea,   a young woman sits thinking,
          she's thinking,
our cross-legged picture-making girl,   of sunrise
          as pink streak,   sunset's a salmon
smear.   Recently post-divorce, she's not sure
          of voids beneath stones   or calm
at that moment when the sun   —   when everything   —   holds back
          in extremis:
breath and fire and nothing we're taught   to believe
          comes true.   Her world's
freight,   bared remorse,   a pale blue cloister
          with red shutters
perched out over the lake's edge, shivering in late autumn's
          grip.   What she loves best
is winter in the real north: *you can do something*
          with it,   she hears herself
think. Years earlier, on honeymoon at Nipigon, the sixth
          great lake in August
reminds her of animals, words without stories, pictures on rocks, not books
          for parsing.   In the night,
snuffling awakens them. Pads molded clean at water's edge in glittering,
          in finest blue-green
particles, reconnoiter the tent, twice around before daylight. She was come for,
          after all,   for she knows
great mammals, upcountry hardwood forests,   tremendous elks' racks
          befriend her.   Lie close, you predators, you prey,
and heavens hold her, envelop her,   palms down pushing brume
          to earth.

The World's Beauties

Single girls in their *do me* heels and halter tops and sprayed-

on jeans   pulsing   shoving and shining all up

     and down the street all eyes   on them

     and knowing it.

—

Pretty lady   in plastic sandals   enchantress of the ordinary

queen of this midday   dusty   shiny   trash-littered anteroom

     you want, want, *want*   him you love   you'll love

     for all your years   to   know *know*   his black-

     haired beauty with eyes like the end   of the day.

—

Old woman, hands folded   over her belly,   looks as if

she grieves the world,   its troubles squirrelled

     away in a woven fray-handled sack,   her gaze

     unwavering.

Rescue

I see you now   as a woman would   internally,

        I know you.

                Raise your hands

To heaven,   beseech and guide,   through jungle foliage,

      through deserts   crossed oceans,

             I know you,

As a woman would with my hands,   your lithe bodies,   filthy

    and fine,   your terrible calm   captive eyes blue and brown,

    and every offer   in between,

        I know you,   I feel you,   as a woman

Would   with hips   and breasts and pitching

       spine.   Pliant rescue   after all these

years   I'm past that now   but still   I speak your names   as a young

    woman would,   sighing.

Old Friend

I am exhausted I am up against the wall   I am up against it in spades
right now   But I have a plan   exciting and I have great
hopes and energy to go   I am ready to go   Last July I got nailed on
drinking while driving   parlayed into   nightmare   So I'm trying
to avoid financial failure   So I'm rethinking   reconsidering my enjoyments
The countdown's going   I have to shake my head   Limited energies to spend
before the   end of the trail   Unbelievably we're almost God-
damned 60   I shake my head   I see people on TV who look really old   and I
find out they are 55 or 61   or something   I stare in disbelief at the me in the
mirror.   It doesn't feel that old in here but   then again   again
          So be careful when you ask   how are you   It's only a matter of
patience and a little bobbing and weaving   Age is the vehicle we all
ride   some times an old familiar   *sometimes*
bumble-footed   we celebrate and cringe   I realize on my good
days   I'm wonderful   and then again   on others
I'm me   just like always

Who I Am

My people gaze stern, swallow
their words, smile without moving
their mouths.

My people seek not redemption
nor God to ease their sorrows
but signs of snow, a warm winter blanket
soothing the land.

My people do not speak of love, the rules
are unrelenting.   And if you say
I love you, they look at you hard,
and venture   nothing.

Old People Remember

One looks me straight in the eye:

I cried when we left California, my brand new ranch
house with the indoor plumbing.   I cried when he drove me

home clear across the country to a dirty farmyard

The other chimes in:
I never wanted all those children, that was what   he wanted.

Old men lower their eyes and study the floor.

—◦◦◦—

Hard And Fierce

When I tell you   *It's not enough,*

     I'm thinking of that animal   in the clear-cut

   that black wobbly-headed

giant   stumbling out   from burnt-over fields,   out   onto the public

road   three good paws, favoring the forth   I saw it as a sign then,

     something   starting   or ending

reckonings hard and fierce   as duty.

     Out on the porch,   a squall approached,   pounding

the distance,   I waited for you to come,

      for you,   for you to show me

   your empty arms your cuts   old scars

I wanted to trace them, then,   their purple furrowed paths;   ill-formed

     streams.   Tangled   the air   stank   of sweat and

   metal   spark and crack   and static.

     Time seemed   longer,   then.

     When I said   *I will always*   you answered

I turned my life upside down,   *tore it*   *apart*   —

The War After

Before dinner, he showed us how he hot-stripped
the woodwork all its layers down to the hand-

planed heart pine   he was certain it was finished
that way,   originally, naked.   I hadn't the heart

to tell him or maybe it was ignorance that so satisfied
coming with his know-it-all-Yankee-this-house-had-

hundreds-of-slaves exaggerations, shames no one
born here   would ever brag on or even

broach.   In the middle of the night it burned
to the ground space heaters caught the damned high-

ceilinged rafters, flames fled the windows that couldn't
reach the sills no matter how hard   you pushed.

—

Bourbon as Southern birthright: he knew how to drink
and taught me, too, sitting on the porch beneath the sky-

painted ceiling after dusk for a while we'd just listen
and rock and sip the night sounds' purred exhaust

—   the owls especially   —   they always know where everything
hides   the pause settling in   before

the beginning and usually, because if it's more or less
true,   it migrates   soul to soul

mouth-to-mouth   moths dashed themselves
nightly to suicide by single bulb   and sometimes

we ended with a question,   a *start*,   the way the best stories
do, my hand caught,   spilling,   midway to mouth.

—

Great-granddaddy from memory: Elmira Prison,
Barracks 3. Hard war is personal. Walk the distance,

half-starved, New York to the Blue Ridge and you'll
know.   Come home to the dead

to find   yourself.   Survive, an outlier.   Carry on.
Make babies. Think about guilt and innocence. Fill up

the emptied rooms the place still set at the table,
hopeful.   Watch as his absence   turns her hating

the survivor for the reminder. Remember, too,
but never speak of it.

Listen as an old blind man   sees.
Stand in for a brother,   never returned.

Pain-scoured White

Alone on a train   through the night   traversing
a desert   I watched fishermen

            mend their nets

            by moonlight

Bright as noon,   and cast them out at glacial prairie,
wind-sanded moraines hot as

            friction,

Each twisted skein   rising
in drift-mantled   hummocks,

            recesses, cleavages, crevices pain-scoured

white and fast   as frozen light.

Touch

Smooth and rich as grassland left alone to eat and drink

     its fill,

Slow and deep: opening a furrow with a moldboard

     plow.

These days I let my hair grow long these luscious   foolish

     days,

I brush it out   for men

     to touch.

There it is   my secret revealed,   crossing Broad in late

     November,

I will, yes,   I will,   I am near.   I am on my way

     on my way.

Pile-up

Stacks,

transparencies   each,

each a single version,   portion, or   plea

piled-up   collapsed

past and present   stuck,   secreted,

tight-pressed,

Illicit partnerships,   jumbled,   faded, blurred   obscured

portraits framed   top and bottom   familiar and

forgotten   side by side, all the way

through.

Walk Away

Everyday phrases   such as   *as you know* and *can't*
continue and *too little*   strip me stake me   alive   a take
for a take,   suspended,   for once

Exposed in open air, sun, past now, this day,
choice,   our souls out for a stroll suffer the commonplace
rue the everyday machinery its

Day-to-day   its unimaginable   its conjuring
unknown   need,   yours for the flesh,   mine for order,
peace of mind,   that cool feeling across my chest,   soul-mending
respite: me   the chill of absence: you.   In exchange:

A two-lane country road, dust-downed arms and legs
covered exactly alike   this time equals,   utterly correct
in our separate   trajectories,   my feet,   broad
and sturdy   take me where I need   to go.

Don't Forgive

Forgiveness bides its time, waits on a ruling.   Rather, incline me to *you just can't win* and *it's the way these things are bound to go.* Turn me towards *I've learned*

My lesson (too late again) remind   absorb   repeat.   I'll admit I knew better but make me

Sturdy again I'm smashed up   again.   But please, no exonerating bystanders;   corpus/head and/or heart we're all   to blame.

—

Last night I watched as snowfall gleamed the filthy streets. This morning's light failed me,   my trespasses,

Transgressions.   There will be scrutiny, yes   scales of
justice,   *yes,*   and judgment.

Him In A Field

You could have been anything   fairy
dust or chiggers in high grass biting
my bare ankles   you could have been
a fawn   a most delicate
creature   lean, muscular   walking
toward me   carefully, closer   cool nose
in my hand   I could have offered you
a biscuit from my pocket   you might have
taken it stared at me until I gave you
more   *I have no more* I might have whispered
turning   walking

Away.   A made-up story at the start
when notes passed for us,   when no other
connection had yet been   made.   Instead,
I might have gathered you held you clutched you
to my chest at this advanced hour when
I should have grasped time's *too late*   and
it's all past and done and   *missed that boat,*
the utter failure of conversation to account for   what   —
disillusionment?   hindsight?
repentance?

You started to pull real
quiet   so I never noticed
your direction, the opposite of mine,   *you,*
you kicked me with all your might
your tiny sharp hoof insistently
strong   —   I gave you all I could think of,
all   I had.

Allemande Hands

When I think of ache   I think

     of you   —   the quit of one

marks   the stay of the other   —   both shortcuts

to a dead end: We've been here

     before,   you and I,

and yet I've learned to follow and you

to lead   or vice versa left

    and right and allemande

hands   touch fingers, clutch fast and

circle,   middle the distance

     pull it   short

wait   a   beat   anticipate

our next position,   hesitate   on best

     behavior   just shy

of ingress   If we can lose

everything and still know   we're familiars

     among strangers   we'll dance

better   together   than we   used to.

Best

Old man, I tucked it all away. I had nowhere else
        to put it.

He laughs when I call him that.   He makes a sound

Like a cello bowing when I tell him   I think we must have saved
        the best   for last.

Farmer

I dream of riches so rich   I could have you   anywhere

I want: in a high-ceilinged Sicilian palazzo,   or burning

up the ice-white torpor of a Greek   late summer   mid-

afternoon.

But I'm only a farmer, exhausted from toil:

I set a modest meal and eat alone in dying light.   I sleep slick

with sweat.   My calloused palms   slough wet

from my breasts.

Even Winds, Pallid Plains

Fireflies glittered bumped carousing   in half-light bodies illumined
signaling   *where are you, I am here, I am here*   without effort

Locating,   rhythmic vibrations,   a midnight   lovers'
resort.   Night skies were black, then, bereft of color   as if

That color, that one is best,   for sadness.   Now it's spark and spangle the

dawn in between   colored joy and touch   and warm.   Now finished,

Ordained and complete,   no openings   anywhere   even winds sweep
pallid plains   fireflies gone,   peepers peeping in another

Time and country   lanterns emptied,   cleaned and tidy, blackbirds

hanging   on a row of nails.

—◡◡◡—

Close

How close we come as we move   through this world.   Cubic inches

of space   we take up,   miles we travel,   mark a distance

between us until we're no longer   certain

whether we're coming   together,   or parting   forever.

The National Federation of State Poetry Societies
Stevens Poetry Manuscript Competition

The National Federation of State Poetry Societies (NFSPS) is a nonprofit organization focused on poetry and education, which sponsors fifty annual poetry contests, the winners of which appear in the anthology *Encore*. NFSPS also sponsors the annual Stevens Poetry Manuscript Competition for the best collection of poems by a single poet. The contest winner receives a cash prize of $1,000, publication by NFSPS Press, and fifty copies of his or her prize-winning book. The annual deadline is October 15th, the decision is announced in January, and the prize-winning book is published in June. Complete submission guidelines are available from the NFSPS website at www.nfsps.com, where winning books and editions of *Encore* can be ordered.

Past Stevens Poetry Manuscript Competition Winners

2013
Breaking Weather, by Betsy Hughes (Rochester Hills, MI: NFSPS Press, 2014). Judge: Glenna Holloway.

2012
Full Cry, by Lisa Ampleman (Rochester Hills, MI: NFSPS Press, 2013). Judge: Maggie Anderson.

2011
Good Reason, by Jennifer Habel (Rochester Hills, MI: NFSPS Press, 2012). Judge: Jessica Garratt.

2010
Lines from the Surgeon's Children, 1862-1865, by Rawdon Tomlinson (Rochester Hills, MI: NFSPS Press, 2011). Judge: Lola Haskins.

2009
Come In, We're Open, by Sara Ries (Rochester Hills, MI: NFSPS Press, 2010). Judge: Ralph Burns.

2008
Bear Country, by Dana Sonnenschein (Rochester Hills, MI: NFSPS Press, 2009). Judge: Carolyne Wright.

2007
Capturing the Dead, by Daniel Nathan Terry (Rochester Hills, MI: NFSPS Press, 2008). Judge: Jeff Gundy.

2006
The Meager Life and Modest Times of Pop Thorndale, by W. T. Pfefferle (Rochester Hills, MI: NFSPS Press, 2007). Judge: Patricia Fargnoli.

2005
Harvest, by Budd Powell Mahan (Rochester Hills, MI: NFSPS Press, 2006). Judge: Lawson Inada.

2004
Aqua Curves, by Karen Braucher (Rochester Hills, MI: NFSPS Press, 2005). Judge: Peter Meinke.

2003
The Zen Piano Mover, by Jeanne Wagner (Rochester Hills, MI: NFSPS Press, 2004). Judge: Ruth Berman.

2002
A Thousand Bonds: Marie Curie and the Discovery of Radium, by Eleanor Swanson (Rochester Hills, MI: NFSPS Press, 2003). Judge: Bruce Eastman.

2001
The Fine Art of Postponement, by Jane Bailey (Rochester Hills, MI: NFSPS Press, 2002). Judge: Donna Salli.

2000

The Stones for a Pillow, by Diane Glancy (Rochester Hills, MI: NFSPS Press, 2001). Judge: David Sutherland.

1999

Binoculars, by Douglas Lawder (Rochester Hills, MI: NFSPS Press, 2000). Judge: Kenneth Brewer.

1998

Singing in the Key of L, by Barbara Nightingale (Rochester Hills, MI: NFSPS Press, 1999). Judge: Sue Brannan Walker.

1997

Weighed in the Balances, by Alan Birkelbach (Austin, TX: Plainview Press, 1998). Judge: Anne Marx.

1996

Shadowless Flight, by Todd Palmer (Deerfield, IL: Lake Shore Publishing, 1997). Judge: Michael Bugeja.

1995

I Have Learned Five Things, by Elaine Christensen (Deerfield, IL: Lake Shore Publishing, 1996). Judge: Michael Dennis Browne.

1994

A Common Language, by Kathryn Clement (Deerfield, IL: Lake Shore Publishing, 1995). Judge: David Baker.